Through the lens: the island of Malta

A photographic essay

Brian Kegels

Copyright © 2018/ Brian Kegels

As well text as photographs are under copyright of the author.

All rights reserved.

ISBN: 9781724182906

TABLE OF CONTENTS

Acknowledgements 1
Introduction 3
Photographic impressions 5
Index of places 103
About the author 105

ACKNOWLEDGEMENTS

I would like to thank Koen for his research, especially of restaurants. Food is important for a man. Also thanks for the making of this book. With his critical eyes he selected the photographs and he evaluated the accompanying text and layout of the book.

Also thanks to Gary for proof reading.

INTRODUCTION

At the far south of Europe, between Italy and the African continent, a group of islands is found known as the Republic of Malta. The main island is also called Malta. It is 27 kilometers (17 miles) long and 14.5 kilometers (9 miles) wide. Malta is Maltese and English speaking (though with an accent).

The international airport is near the city of Luqa. It is reached from London in a 3.5 hour flight and from Brussels in a 3 hour flight. The airport has car rental services. Malta is left hand driving. Roads on the countryside are bumpy. Public transport buses take you all over the island.

Malta has its knights, its capital Valletta, palaces and fortresses and the coastal life.
Valletta is the main city and capital. Birgu is glued to it. The silent city of Mdina is landsinwards. The rest of the island is rural or industrial with occasionally a big or small village. Around the island are bays, ports, sandy and rocky beaches, salt pans, cliffs and caves.

Photographers have nice coastal and architectural sights. Valletta offers attractions visited by many tourists. Mdina is great for ancient city photography, since it is less crowded. Malta also has remains of pre-Roman temples. Take precautions against the sun concerning your camera, skin, hydration and eyes. In summer, temperature rises easily to 30 °C (86 °F) and rain is exceptional. Valletta streets go up and down.

This book contains photographs of the island of Malta. The focus is on the photos. They give beautiful impressions and are provided with a short explanation and different kinds of facts. Mostly it includes the location. In this way readers can create their itinerary having stops at places they are interested in.
So, this book is not a traveler's guide.

The photos in this book are taken by the author himself in Valletta, Birgu, Mdina and Rabat, at the countryside and on sea. The details of the locations are listed in the index of places at the end of this book.

PHOTOGRAPHIC IMPRESSIONS

Being saluted in Valletta

The Upper Barracca Gardens offer a stunning view of Valletta, the Grand Harbour, and the three cities. The three cities are Birgu, Cospicua, and Senglea. They are located across the Grand Harbour.

The canons that make part of the saluting battery are set on Upper Barracca Gardens. Sometimes one of them is fired.

Harbour of Birgu

The city of Birgu is often called Vittoriosa. It is one of the three cities and can be seen from Valletta. A regular public boat service operates between the harbour of Birgu and Valletta. It is not expensive and the use of the elevator to Upper Barracca Gardens is included. Outside high season the ferry ends early on the day (verify operating hours accurately). A bus service is an alternative.

View on Lower Barracca Gardens

Valletta is located on a peninsula in the shape of the letter V. In the middle of it towards the opening the elevation gets quickly higher. Lower Barracca Gardens is situated halfway to the point of the V. It has a public park with nice view over sea, harbour and the cities.

Dromedary in Republic Street

Republic Street is the best known street and splits Valletta through the middle. Parts of the street are only for pedestrians. Most constructions are built with the light brown Maltese limestone. The stone is easy to carve and sculpt.

The decorations of many buildings are marvelous to see. One of the sculpted decorations is a coat of arms having a dromedary in the middle.

Buzz near the square

The galleries of the Bibliotheca on Republic Square in Valletta give shelter against the sun. At this cool spot one can hear the buzz coming from the cafés on the square.

Grandmaster's palace corridor

The Grandmaster's palace in Valletta is built starting of the sixteenth century. The Grandmaster of the Knights Hospitaller housed here. Currently the president of Malta has his residence in the palace.

Many decorations are trompe l'oeil, painted seeming to be real. The light falling into the corridor's end is beautifully illuminating the doors, the walls, and the steps.

Guarding armors

The Grandmaster's palace in Valletta is worth visiting because of its state rooms, the decoration, and the armory. Breathtaking are the unique tapestries picturing exotic scenes hanging in the Tapestry Hall.

The palace has many marble floors. The walls and ceilings are painted in diverse motives. In the corridors stand suits of armor nicely on a row.

Guggling eagle

Hearing the running water of the fountain at Saint George's Square in Valletta relaxes. The water bursts out of the beak of an eagle and the mouth of a man's head and drops into the basin beneath.

Marble art floors

The floors of palaces and churches laid with marble are amazing. The stones with the perfect color are precisely cut and laid in the complex jigsaw puzzle.
The floors depict coats of arms or symmetric figures.

Next to the top of Victoria Gate

In the past Victoria gate was the main entrance to the city of Valletta from the Grand Harbour. People can walk as well through as over the gate. The top of the gate is most interesting for taking photos.

Leaning lion

At Archbishop Street near Lower Barracca Gardens in Valletta leans this lion on an escutcheon. The steps beside it lead up to Republic Street and afterwards down to Marsamxett Harbour.

Boring outside, astonishing inside

The exterior of the Saint John's Co-Cathedral in Valletta is tight, plain, almost boring. This is in contrast with the interior, which is richly decorated. The ceiling is fully painted. Walls carry gold-plated stucco. The complete floor is laid with marble tombs stones and marble designs.

It shares the function of cathedral together with the one of Mdina.

Gold-plated details on the arches

The arches of the Saint John's Co-Cathedral of Valletta carries many details and is largely gold-plated.

In case of a service only a small part of the cathedral is freely accessible.

Passing Ricasoli

This cruise ship passes Fort Ricasoli and enters Grand Harbour. Valletta is surrounded by many forts to protect against invasions of foreign countries or pirates. Some of the forts can be visited, such as Fort Saint Elmo, Fort Saint Angelo and Fort Rinella.

Bay windows

These flats have wooden bay windows painted in different colors and are exposed to the natural elements of sea water, wind, precipitation and sun.

Birgu marina

The public ferry service from Birgu to Valletta and back passes the marina and Fort Saint Angelo. It stops near the Bormla bus stop in Birgu and arrives at the elevator of Upper Barracca Gardens in Valletta.

Welcomed by a bull

Birgu marina has a nice promenade to Fort Saint Angelo. At the other end of the promenade is a limestone gate. On top of it a bull's head is placed, seemingly welcoming every visitor to the marina.

Stair case in Inquisitor's Palace

The Inquisitor's Palace in Birgu is a construction that is systematically extended. It housed the inquisitor of the Catholic church, the inquisitor's tribunal and prisons.

The palace has beautiful architectural parts such as the staircase. View the painted ceiling, the bright light through the windows, and the limestone walls and railing.

Balustrade

The white light rays on this railing with balusters and drops shades in the room. Photographically, the picture has a few lines and a repetition of balusters.

Sailing past the salt pans

When passing along the shores, the salt pans at the coast will be noticed. Most of them are still used to win salt from the sea water that flooded into the pans.

Cactus flowers

Vegetation often seen on Malta is the cactus. Its flowers are mostly yellow or pink. The climate of warm dry summers and mild winters is ideal for cactus plants.

Whole in the peninsula

The southeast of Malta has a few small bays ideal for walking, swimming, sunbathing or taking pictures. A little peninsula named Ras il-Fniek near Marsaxlokk has a small opening under it.

Saint Peter's salt pans

Saint Peter's pool near Marsaxlokk is a small bay with a little beach called Saint Peter's pool. Close to it are a few salt pans. From the top of the cliff a rocky trail leads around the bay down to sea level.

Longing for bees

The caper grows on rocky surfaces. It has big white flowers with long purple stamens longing for bees. The caper flowers and its berries seem to be edible, though poisonous species also exist.

Luzzus on the water

Hundreds of small boats lie on the water in the little harbour of Marsaxlokk. The traditional fisher boats with bright colors usually red, blue and yellow are called luzzus. On each side of the front of the boats an eye is painted, which is believed to protect the fishermen.

Marsaxlokk is a small fisher town having many restaurants and cafés at the promenade along the harbour.

Coastal chapel

Next to the main road in the small village of Wied iz-Zurrieq stands a tiny chapel. Wied iz-Zurrieq means valley of Zurrieq and is located at the seaside.

Sundown at the southern coastline

The coastline at the south of Malta is rocky, and at some places has steep cliffs. The endless views over the sea and the disappearing sun are magnificent.

The Blue Grotto Boat Service

Wied iz-Zurrieq is the main departure for excursions to the Blue Grotto. In an inlet of the sea, boats wait in the little port of the village to carry tourists along the rocky coast line. The boat service organizes a limited number of trips to the Blue Grotto.

Heading to the Blue Grotto

Along the shores the boats with tourists navigate to the Blue Grotto. The excursion lasts for less than 30 minutes, but is a fun and refreshing experience.
Photographers must watch out for splashing water on their camera.

Caves in the cliffs

The coastline near Wied iz-Zurrieq offers a palette of colors. The water has many shades of blue. The rocks at sea level are green, mauve, red and orange due to corals and algae. The white and light brown limestone cliffs show glowing reflections of the blue water. At higher levels the cliffs are covered with green vegetation.

Some caves in the cliffs are illuminated with an azure glow by reflections of the light blue surface under the water.

Taking the boat and moving close to the meters high rocks is adventurous. Natural erosion have carved many shapes in the rocks of Maltese limestone.

Inside the cave

In the cliffs near Wied iz-Zurrieq are numerous caves. Excursion boats enter some of them. Temperature and light decrease quickly. The sound of the waves echoes on the walls.

Leg of rock

Blue Grotto can be described as a massive rock sticking out of the cliffs having a leg of rock standing in the sea water. It has an opening towards the sea and behind another one directing to the cliffs.

Blue Grotto of Wied iz-Zurrieq

Blue grotto is the major touristic attraction of Wied iz-Zurrieq. The excursion boats navigate in it. From above it can be admired from a view point near the main road. It has many wide views over the small valley, the rocks at each end of the valley, and the Mediterranean Sea.

White cliffs of Dingly

Excellent for walking, sightseeing and photographing are the Dingly cliffs. Especially at the northwest of Dingly along the shore are many hiking trails. From the top of the cliffs are endless views over the sea. The cliffs are white and steep. Hear the water splashing to them.

Ghajn Tuffieha bay

Malta has few sandy beaches. In the northwest of the island the Ghajn Tuffieha beach can be found in a small bay. It can only be reached by sea or a long walk down the stairs. Around it are other bays with beaches and walking trails.

Saint Agatha catacombs

The city of Rabat has so called catacombs, underground burial places dug out in the limestone during the Roman time. The catacombs of Saint Paul are well visited by tourists. The catacombs of Saint Agatha just across the street are smaller, more intimate and more authentic.

The lions of Mdina main gate

The city of Mdina is entered by its main gate. First visitors must pass a bridge with a lion holding an escutcheon on each side of it. The whole construction is of Maltese limestone. Noteworthy is that the entrance was moved a few meters to the left during a reconstruction.

Silence in the narrow streets

Mdina is called the silent city, only cars with a permit are allowed into it. Often a horse drawn carriage rides through the silent streets. Mdina does not know the stress that other cities are subjected to.

Strolling through the city's narrow streets during the day or in the evening is pleasurable because of the tranquility and the silence. Remark the detailed decorations that many houses have, such as a metal ornament on the door.

City with historic charm

Mdina already exists since Roman time. The many buildings are churches and former palaces of nobility. The historic street lights are still hanging. This combination gives the city a visual charm, which can be exploited as a photographer.

Mdina portal

Many residents of Mdina have a richly decorated front of their house. Often the coat of arms of the person living in the palace is carved in the stone of the portal, or it is attached to it.

Historic street lights

In the streets of Mdina historic street lights are still installed. The lights have details that are enlarged by the shadows, such as the pins of the fixation of it.

Flower house

Also vegetation is used as a decoration for resident's houses. A house partly covered with climbing plants, heavily blossoming purple flowers.

Everything below Mdina

Mdina is situated on a raised surface. On the city walls of Mdina you have a nice look down to the surrounding landscape. In the east the Mediterranean Sea and the bordering cities including Valletta are located.

Mdina cathedral

From a far distance, Mdina can be recognized by the dome and two towers of the Saint Paul's Cathedral. Similar to the Saint John's Co-Cathedral of Valletta, it is richly decorated with marble, frescos and gold-plated stucco. It also has marvelous tombstones throughout the floor.

INDEX OF PLACES

Archbishop Street, Valletta

Bibliotheca galleries, National Library, Republic Square, Valletta
Birgu marina, promenade and gate, Xatt il-Forn, Birgu
Blue Grotto Boat Service, ticket booth near port of Wied iz-Zurrieq
Blue Grotto viewpoint, Wied iz-Zurrieq Street (bus stop Panorama), Wied iz-Zurrieq

Dingly cliffs, Triq Panoramika, Dingly

Fort Ricasoli, view from Valletta
Fort Rinella, Kalkara
Fort Saint Angelo, Xatt Il-Forn, Birgu
Fort Saint Elmo, Valletta

Ghajn Tuffieha bay, Riviera, Mgarr
Grandmaster's palace, Palace Square, Valletta

Inquisitor's Palace, Birgu

Lower Barracca Gardens, Valletta

Marsaxlokk, bays, Xrobb I-Ghagin Nature Park

Marsaxlokk, promenade and port
Mdina main gate, Mdina Road
Mdina Cathedral, Saint Pauls Cathedral, Saint Paul Street 2, Mdina
Mdina walls, Bastion Square, Mdina

Ras il-Fniek, Marsaxlokk
Republic Street, Valletta
Republic Square, Valletta

Saint Agatha catacombs, Saint Agatha Street, Rabat
Saint George's Square, Valletta
Saint John's Co-Cathedral, Republic Street (visitor's entrance) or Saint Paul Street (main entrance), Valletta
Saint Paul's catacombs, Saint Agatha Street, Rabat
Saint Peter's pool and salt pans, Marsaxlokk

Upper Barracca Gardens and elevator, Valletta

Victoria Gate, Liesse Street, Valletta

Wied iz-Zurrieq chapel, Congreve Street, Wiez iz-Zurrieq

ABOUT THE AUTHOR

Brian Kegels was born in 1978 in Antwerp (Belgium). In his professional life he is an independent analyst describing business processes and functionalities for software projects.

During many years he has travelled often in Europe, Asia and America. Photography, gastronomy, nature, history and culture are the centerpieces of these travels. Traveling the world is adventure that broadens your mind.

The author has a portfolio of photographs. They are published to be printed on a canvas or to be framed. The author can be contacted for questions or to buy (framed) pictures by sending an e-mail to throughthelens@telenet.be.

Made in the USA
Lexington, KY
14 February 2019